I WILL ARISE THIS DAY

I WILL ARISE THIS DAY

Melissa Musick Nussbaum

Art by Kristen Anderson

LITURGY TRAINING PUBLICATIONS

Also by Melissa Musick Nussbaum: *I Will Lie Down This Night*

This book was designed by Jill Smith. Gabe Huck was the editor, and Deborah Bogaert was the production editor. Typesetting was by Jim Mellody-Pizzato, in Goudy. The book was printed and bound by BookCrafters of Chelsea, Michigan.

Library of Congress Cataloging-in-Publication Data
Nussbaum, Melissa Musick.
    I will arise this day / Melissa Musick Nussbaum ; art by Kristen Anderson.
        p.   cm.
    1. spiritual life — Catholic Church. 2. Prayer. 3. Christian life — Catholic authors. 4. Christian biography. 5. Christmas — Meditations. I. Title.
    BX2350.2.N87   1996
    242 — dc20   96-20695
                                                                                        CIP

ISBN 1-56854-135-X
ARISE

CONTENTS

To Andrew D. Ciferni, OPRAEM.
Mentor, teacher, faithful friend

How good to thank you, Lord,
to praise your name, Most High,
to sing your love at dawn . . .
For your work brings delight,
your deeds invite song.

—*Psalm 92:2 – 3, 5*

But I cry out to you, God,
each morning I plead with you.

—*Psalm 88:14*

Foreword

Wouldn't there be some fascinating reading at the end of our lives if each morning upon awakening we entered our first thoughts into a journal? Here would be the hopes and fears for the day before us, our thanks and praise for the blessings of a new day and our petitions for our own and others' needs.

The psalms often refer to the prayer that takes place upon our beds. There is a particular intimacy and honesty in the conversation that takes place between us and God as we drift off to sleep at the end of one day and as we begin to stir at the beginning of the next.

Prayer in the morning is wired into the human psyche. It may not carry the label "prayer." We may discover it in the affections that accompany a drive up an incline such as Mount Cadillac in Maine to see the first rays of the sun touch the easternmost shore of the continental United States, or a predawn hike up Mount Sinai to view the desert coming into color as the source of all daylight rises in the heavens. We may find it in looking out the window on a winter morning to see if the first rays of the dawn will give evidence of a "snow day." It may surprise us in the thoughts that come to mind as we brush our teeth and find ourselves praying for wisdom in the class we must teach or the homily we will preach. We must be familiar with it as we clatter around the kitchen or as we drive or ride into the city for another day's work.

Prayer in the morning was taught to us at our mother's knee before we knew the meaning of the words we were committing to memory. Melissa Nussbaum, a mother and leader of prayer, makes a second contribution to praying in and through time. She gives us a primer for morning prayer grounded in a down-to-earth awareness of the movements of the Spirit which grace our first waking moments and hours. This needs its place on the nightstand or with our Bible or volume of the Liturgy of the Hours. Its prayers are best used and its chapters best read before we open the morning papers or listen to the news. One chapter a week might be enough for a start. Reread the same chapter several days in a row and pause at the end to note the movements of heart and mind that are suggested by what you've read.

Those coming fresh to morning prayer might want to begin with a simple pattern of prayer drawn from the collection at the end of this little book. Again, one prayer repeated each day for a week might be enough. The goal here, as in our early childhood, is to commit the prayer to heart. The essays help us explore the movements of the Spirit that are particular to each day's beginning and which, when lifted to God on our bed, in our chair, on our knees, in our kitchen or automobile, on a plane, a train, or a mountaintop, give us direction toward the day's middle and its end.

Andrew D. Ciferni, OPRAEM.

CHAPTER 1

RISING INTO FULLNESS

Almighty God, Creator,
The morning is yours, rising into fullness.

— George MacLeod

We keep the feast of St. Nicholas. No lentil soup or leftover casserole appears on the table on December 6. We eat in the dining room on, if not damask, then a passable imitation of it, with cloth napkins, the "good" china and our wedding silver, which must be washed afterward by hand.

At some point near the end of the meal, the doorbell rings. My husband and I sternly admonish the children, "stay seated," but all of them, even the older ones, rush to the door in the hope of seeing the good saint as he makes his rounds through the darkness of Advent. All they ever find is a letter addressed to the five of them.

The letter from St. Nicholas is a reflection on the year that ended with the feast of Christ the King. It is filled with gentle exhortations: to love God more, day by day; to grow in wisdom, in stature and in grace; to become, as David was, a creature after the Creator's own heart. And it is filled with broad hints as to how those ends might best be achieved: Biting was strongly discouraged for many years, and with little effect; hitting, tattling and screaming "I hate you!" as a way of initiating dialogue have also, from year to year, been considered by the dear saint and rejected as reliable paths to either holiness or good communication. At the end of the letter, St. Nicholas offers clues — in the form of a simple rhyme — to the

whereabouts of the sack of small gifts and candies he has left. It is,
our Mary Margaret says, her favorite feast of the year.

Some years ago, on the morning of December 6, I was in the kitchen preparing the evening feast when the phone rang. A young woman I knew, a woman I'll call Angela, was on the line sobbing, telling me that her estranged husband had broken into her apartment. He had beaten her in front of their three small children, then walked away. She was afraid he would return to finish his bloody work. Could she, she asked, gather up the children and come to my house, where they would be hidden, where they would be warm and safe?

My first, unspoken response was an irritated "No." I was sifting the flour three separate times for a particularly tricky cake recipe.

I was planning how I would accomplish the illusion of domestic order before nightfall. I was getting ready to celebrate the feast day of the patron saint of children.

Whatever my desires, I knew that the patron saint of children probably desired shelter for Angela and her children over scratch cake. So with neither a pure heart nor a willing spirit, I said, "Yes. Of course. Come. Come quickly." And they came, Angela bruised and swelling, the children each clutching some treasure he or she had snatched from the wreckage of their home as they fled. The older boy, James, cradled an electronic game, its sharp plastic edges poking his bony arms, its disconnected cord trailing behind him as he walked through the door. I remember thinking, from the safe side of the front door, that this was a curious choice for a child who was without a place to plug it in. They had it all wrong, these untidy people with their untidy lives.

My feast day plans fell apart. The house got dirtier. The food sat, raw, in the refrigerator. We had to find a doctor for Angela. We had to feed her children. We had to maintain contact with the police, who were searching for her husband. We had to find a place where Angela and her children could live safely while they plotted their next moves.

It was only later that I considered how much Angela was like Mary that day: weary and in need of shelter in a city where it seemed that every door was shut to her and to the little ones in her care. It was only later that I thought of their journey from their apartment to our house to the safe house as being like that more famous journey, the flight from Bethlehem into Egypt and safety.

What I considered that day was how my plans, my assumptions for a day that always ran a certain way, were being disrupted and sucked in by this woman. Yet even in my anger and impatience, I knew, I knew to be true what I told the children when we finally sat down at the table: "This isn't the day I had planned. I suspect it was the day St. Nicholas had planned. I hope he was pleased with our celebration."

Morning prayer is about assumptions, the assumptions with which we begin each day, every day, and so, our lives. After a concealed weapons ban was repealed in Colorado Springs, *Time* magazine ran a picture of a local prohandgun councilwoman. The photo

was a close-up of her manicured fingers slipping a small pistol into a
purse. "How is it," I wondered when I saw that picture, "to wake and
dress and walk into the morning with the assumption that I will meet
someone today who needs shooting?" And how is it to wake and
dress and walk into the morning assuming that I am the one who
must shoot? The assumptions of the morning claim the rest of the
day — the armed person who meets a stranger isn't looking for
angels unawares but for marauders, and she has already decided, by
loading and carrying the gun, who the stranger is and how she will
treat the stranger. It is in her power to make that choice.

Morning prayer asks us to consider a very different set of
assumptions. Listen to the words from the invitatory Psalm 95:

A great God is the Lord,
over the gods like a king.
God cradles the depths of the earth,
holds fast the mountain peaks.
God shaped the ocean and owns it,
formed the earth by hand.

Come, bow down and worship,
kneel to the Lord our maker.
This is our God, our shepherd,
we are the flock led with care.

"A great God is the Lord/over the gods like a king." To sit with
morning prayer is to acknowledge the One greater than all the
household gods: of fear and loathing and greed and envy, of the need
to make every choice and so control every person and every situa-
tion. Yet surrendering needs and acknowledging another are choices
themselves, an exercise of another kind of control; this is more radical still. To recognize that the One who shaped the ocean owns it
is to recognize who owns the day as well. Ownership is a powerful
American concept. "It's my property; I paid for it" translates through-
out the land as "Back off; no trespassing." In proclaiming this psalm
we surrender power; we rearrange ourselves — are rearranged — by
the very words: no longer owner, leader or even rugged individual-
ist. God is our shepherd, and we are part of the flock God leads with

care. No lamb was ever in the ruling class. Lambs are led and fed, receivers of action rather than its initiators. To sit with morning prayer is to begin the day with a radically different set of assumptions than those with which we awoke. Most of us wake up with a daily agenda: all that must be overseen and undertaken for ourselves and our families. The only agenda of Psalm 95 is this one: "Come, bow down and worship."

I awaken most mornings mindful of someone who needs shooting. Given that I don't own a gun, I have to use whatever other legal weapons are available. I am handiest with a sharp word, and I know how to draw blood from tender, hidden places. Morning prayer demands that I put away my weapons as I put away my assumptions for the day and accept God's instead. Morning prayer demands that

I relinquish my desire, my need, to plot and plan each thought, each movement of the children in my keeping. If God formed the earth, the mountains I see outside my window, by hand, then surely God, and not I, formed my children. They are God's — as is, morning prayer reminds me, everything I will see or touch or smell or hear or taste this day and everyone I will meet this day. In morning prayer I begin the day with empty hands, emptied of weapons, of expecta-tions, of the deeds I draw up again and again on the lives of those around me.

I do not like to remember how close I came, how much I wanted to turn Angela away on that feast of St. Nicholas. I do not care to remember how I valued my assumptions for the day before her life and the lives of her children. I choose to recall the story with myself as the heroine, the intrepid rescuer of battered women, but it is not true. My assumptions, if allowed to stand, could have done every bit as much damage as any gun.

How do we learn to put aside our assumptions? How do we learn to begin the day bowed low and reverent? How do we learn anything? Colorado Springs is the home of the Olympic Training Center. No magic happens there; what does happen is people doing the same thing over and over — running sprints, lifting weights, swimming laps until they are changed, shaped and molded into athletes who can move faster and farther than before. I never imagined I would spend so much of my adult life nagging, saying the same things over and over again: "Ask nicely. Pick up your socks. Put your plate in the sink." But that is how we learn. We learn to begin the day bowed low and reverent by bowing, low and reverently, and by praying every morning, in the simple and ancient words, in the simple and ancient way, day after day, the praises of God:

My God,
I pray that I may so know you and love you
    that I may rejoice in you.
And if I may not do so fully in this life,
    let me go steadily on
    to the day when I come to that fullness.
    Let me receive
That which you promised through your truth,
    that my joy may be full.

— St. Anselm

LORD, OPEN MY LIPS

I will kindle my fire this morning
In the presence of the holy angels of heaven.
God kindle thou in my heart within
A flame of love to my neighbor,
To my foe, to my friend, to my kindred all.
To the brave, to the knave, to the thrall,
O Son of the loveliest Mary,
O Son of the loveliest Mary,
From the lowliest thing that liveth
To the Name that is highest of all.

— traditional Celtic prayer

Every summer we spend a week at a camp high in the San Juan Mountains of Colorado. It is cold there, even on summer mornings, and we awaken to the first frost-revealing light under piles of woolen blankets. Our only source of heat in the cabin is a wood-burning stove. Either my husband or I kindle the fire, placing slivers of wood scraps and balls of crumpled newspaper into the cold belly of the stove. It is slow work, cold work; we do it grudgingly. "Martin," I whisper, "it's time for you to get up and make the fire." And so begins, *sotto voce,* the domestic duel of the one who did the supper dishes versus the one who took Andrew on a midnight trek to the bathhouse. I rise, or he rises, the loser uncurling, grumbling, from a cocoon of cotton and wool but soon shocked into speed and silence by the still, frigid air. Strike the match, tend the spark; the builder is careful lest the growing pile of kindling smother the meager flame that leaps from stick to stick, licking the print and pictures from wrinkled pages and leaving behind only the dancing ash.

How cold it has grown in the cabin while we slept. Night stole away the warmth we had gathered, a theft we fail to notice in our thermostat-driven home in the city. But here in the mountains, we know: Nighttime shelters a killing cold, and the kindling of the morning fire dispels the chill and shelters us, the living.

The flame in the stove plays along its iron walls, coloring them with heat's hues. A change in the air, a stirring, rouses the sleepers from their slumber. They hear the hiss of the kettle as it rocks on the hot metal of the stove. They smell the mingled perfume of woodsmoke and oil spitting in the pan. Sounds and smells alert them to a warmth that has not yet reached the far corners of the cabin. They are drawn from bed, but they do not disperse, do not scatter for showers or fishing or to graze among the groceries. Back in the city, morning is a private affair: this one listening to the radio station where John Lennon never dies, that one to the television news where death is omnipresent. We are separated by our worries and our calendars, calculating even as we wake what must be done and when. In the mountains we gather. We come to the fire, close enough to stay within the circle of heat but distant enough, just distant enough, to escape burning. There, we know nothing will begin until the warmth has soaked through our skins.

So we all sit around the fire, recounting dreams that begin to dissipate in the heat and in the telling, rubbing sleep from our eyes and stretching sleep from our uncurling bodies. We are drawn by warmth to warmth, by light to light, and there we gather.

Light and its warmth gladdens and draws us all. Every parent who has ever walked the night with a sick or crying baby knows the relief that dawn brings. It is not that the fever is broken or the colic soothed, it is that morning has broken: The world is awake, and we are still alive in it. The pediatrician will soon be in her office. The pharmacist will soon be in his shop. Help is near at hand.

I remember a night soon after our daughter Anna Kate was born. She refused rest and pulled me with her through the moist infant landscape of soiled gowns and wet diaper mounds. I fed her, rocked her, sang to her and reasoned with her. I begged her to sleep and finally cried with her. My husband had an exam the next morning; he was sorry and sympathetic, but could I please take the baby to another room so he could get some rest? Anna Kate, rooting, would find my breast and suckle herself into sleep. Once her lips grew slack around the nipple she would startle, wide-eyed, and begin again her fretful wails.

We watched morning spread over the city, Anna Kate and I, rocking and weeping our exhausted tears. Martin got the older children and himself off to school. I settled Mary Margaret before the television, hoping to dull her sharp and rested senses into a state more like my own. I held on to the thought that my sister Marilyn had promised to drive over that day and help. Then I looked out the window and saw her: my sister, come with strong arms, patient arms, to hold the baby who had grown so heavy in my own. I could release Anna Kate, fold my hands and let them rest. As I lay down, sweet sleep washing me from the gritty shore into the dreaming waves, I thought about my father, opening his breakfast paper and turning first, as was his custom, to the obituary page. "Just checking," he always said, "just checking." To have survived the night is a wonder.

We acknowledge in morning prayer the miracle of daily light and everyday life begun again: "the great joy," Dietrich Bonhoeffer calls it, that all people, in all places, "feel every morning at the return of the light." Our lips can open, our eyes can see, our ears can hear. Our beds did not become our tombs; night did not prevail. The light has scattered the darkness, and we lie awake in its glow. From the earliest days of our community, Christians have greeted the day with the prayer of praise. In morning prayer we are invited to gather in the light, to bask in the warmth of the rekindled fire. We are invited to begin nothing until the day has soaked into our skins, until the Lord has opened our lips to sing praise:

You are a fire, ever burning and never consumed.
You are a light, ever shining and never fading.
You are goodness beyond all goodness,
Beauty beyond all beauty,
Wisdom beyond all wisdom.
You are the garment that covers all nakedness.
You are the food that satisfies all hunger.

— St. Catherine of Siena

CHAPTER 3

AND MY MOUTH WILL PROCLAIM YOUR PRAISE

O God, early in the morning I cry to you.
Help me to pray, and to concentrate my thoughts on you:
I cannot do this alone.

Restore me to liberty,
And enable me so to live now
that I may answer before you and before me.
Lord, whatever this day may bring,
Your name be praised.

— Dietrich Bonhoeffer

In 1970, when I was eighteen, I left Texas for Germany to spend a year as an exchange student with the Rittner family in Stuttgart. Frau Rittner's mother, Sophie, lived in the house. She was, it seemed to me, very old, a refugee from the reality of the twentieth century. Nearly 30 years before, her two sons, teenagers even younger than I was then, had been conscripted. They were taken from school, one after the other, and sent to the eastern front, where the boys disappeared. No bodies were ever returned to Sophie, but a state photographer did come on two separate occasions to record her receiving the news that her son was "missing and presumed dead." Photos of stoic mothers were thought to be morale builders, her daughter told me. She doubted that the pictures of her own mother, screaming, sobbing, flailing her arms at the spying cameras, were of much use. It wasn't just the deaths, Frau Rittner said of her mother's grief, it was the rumors of cannibalism coming west with every trainload of casualties.

I had been raised not to address my elders by their first names. "Sophie" felt strange on my ma'am-trained tongue. But I could not call her otherwise, for soon after my arrival, she became convinced that we were sisters. I was "Natalie," and she, of course, was Sophie. Not the Sophie who had lived through the deaths of her sons, but

her younger self, living in a world that knew nothing of trench war-
fare or firebombing. We walked together in the late afternoons, arm
in arm, and she would chide me for greeting each passerby. "Do you
know that man, Natalie?" she would whisper. I always shook my head
no. "What will he think?" she would finish reprovingly.

Home again, we brushed one another's hair. We sat on the
sofa near the pictures of her boys, now strangers to a woman who
had willed herself out of the births that would end in slaughter.

I welcomed Sophie's company, in part because she spoke the
German of a small child and I could understand her. Broken objects
were always "kaput" — a baby word, Herr Rittner reminded me, not
the word of an educated person — and sick people were always
"krank," whether the malady was laryngitis or leukemia. Sophie,

waiting at the table, winked at me and, grabbing her knife and fork like stanchions, pounded on the wood, chanting *"Hunger haben wir! Hunger haben wir!"* And I joined in my kindergarten Deutsch.

With youthful presumption, I found Sophie odd: somewhat pathetic but kind, a combination I thought I knew well from my own family. I never thought she was brave until that winter when news came from home. My father, who had gone into the hospital for open-heart surgery, was dying. Frau Rittner helped me pack for the flight to Texas, adding her own string bag of good chocolate and cheese, hard bread and salami. She did not share the American faith in vacuum-packed peanuts and canned sodas as sustenance for the journey, and she knew I had a very long way to go.

Herr Rittner was to drive me to the airport, so I said my good-byes at the house. We had decided to say nothing to Sophie, who would surely find another pleasant memory to inhabit. But Sophie came down the stairs, carrying her rose-gold confirmation ring. She put it on my finger and hugged me close, murmuring, "Poor little girl. Poor little thing. So far from home and her Papa so ill."

What I know now is that I witnessed an act of great courage. Sophie — at the cost of what tearing pain as she passed, and saw, her sons' pictures on the way out the door — forced herself into the present to see me. She saw me as I was, a foreign guest and not her vanished Natalie. She reemerged into a world too cruel for habitation that she might hold me, comfort me and give me a talisman for the journey — a talisman I keep to this day. I never saw Sophie or any of the Rittners again. I am sure Sophie is long dead. But I remember her and think of the price she paid to leave the comfortable fantasy home of her Herr Vater and Frau Mutter to join me in my grief.

There is always a cost to real presence, to attention that admits no happy diversions, no comfortable lies. To sit in silence, to allow the morning to soak into our slumber-drenched skin, to shun the distracting sounds of radio and television, requires courage. To listen to one's own heartbeat is to hear still the skipped rhythms, the racing pulse. To listen to the heartbeat of the house is to sense still the unresolved angers, the wounds yet raw and the ones that have begun to fester. To listen to the heartbeat of the world is to know what drove Sophie into a changeless past where her greatest worry was of seeming fresh and forward to strange men on the street.

There is always a cost to praise. The opening words of morning prayer, "Lord, open my lips, and my mouth will proclaim your praise," suggest the difficulty. "Lord [you do it — they implore], open my lips," for as Dietrich Bonhoeffer confessed from his prison cell, "I cannot do this alone." The very grammar acknowledges the difficulty of praise in the face of the distinctly unpraiseworthy facts.

Bonhoeffer praised God from the cell he knew he would never leave alive. What, then, could his petition "Restore me to liberty" mean? Perhaps by liberty Bonhoeffer meant the freedom to praise, the openness to declare a mercy hidden like seed beneath frozen soil. What folly to look out on a February landscape and expect in just a few weeks to see crocus and daffodils there. What foolishness to look out from barred windows and sing of freedom. What madness to open the morning paper, with its solemn reportage of predatory youth, killers so young they wouldn't be allowed on some amusement park roller coasters, and believe that the God of Israel comes to set us free. We cannot do this alone.

I remember the fairy tale of the elves who stole each night into the home of the poor shoemaker. While the family slept, the elves cut and sewed fine leather boots for the shoemaker to sell. Rereading the story as a mother, I noticed what I missed as a child: The elves not only generated income, they picked up after themselves. It is a wholly satisfying tale for a middle-aged woman who, though no longer waiting for her prince to come, still yearns to wake and find the world — from her kitchen outward in ever-spreading circles — washed clean.

Of course it never is. The overdraft we argued about after dinner remains overdrawn. The lump in the breast detected in the bedtime shower is there in the morning. The child who went to sleep angry with you wakes up angry and, worse, refreshed to fight again.

Even on ordinary mornings, mornings devoid of the drama of war or death or desertion, there is domestic muck to step in and wade through as soon as one crawls out of bed. Our Elisabeth, a grudging early riser, and her younger sister, Mary Margaret, who begrudges rising at all, were bound by ties of convenience — ours — in an unhappy carpool all through their years together in high school. They battled in the bathroom and at the breakfast table, hostilities reaching their daily climax when, at 6:50, Elisabeth, who was ready, threatened Mary Margaret, who was not, with leaving. From time to time she made good on the threat.

I know what it is to steel oneself to rise. I know what it is to lie under the covers and wish for a day other than the one that awaits. That day — the day on which I am richer and thinner and lauded and loved by all — is the day I can begin with praise.

And yet we are told — not counseled, not requested — to declare the praise of God every morning. We declare the praise of God not because the elves have come in the night but in light of the reality that they have not, have never, and will never, come. We declare the praise of God in light of faith's reality that Christ has come and is even now setting the captives free, opening the eyes of

the blind, lifting up the hearts of those who mourn. In the mess and
hurry of the morning, Christians praise God.

"Our ritual prayer," Gabe Huck writes, "binds us to the world as it is. It may be filled with the works of darkness, with hardship, hurt, sadness, ingratitude, frustration, but morning's prayer proclaims that praise which knows God's love will prevail." Morning's prayer proclaims with all the living that which cannot be contained, that which must be declared:

May none of God's wonderful works keep silence,
   night or morning.
Bright stars, high mountains, the depths of the seas,
   sources of rushing rivers:
May all these break into song as we sing
   to the Father, Son, and Holy Spirit.
May all the angels in the heavens reply:
   Amen, amen, amen.
   Power, praise, honour, eternal glory to God,
   To the only giver of grace,
   Amen, amen, amen.

— Anonymous, fourth century

CHAPTER 4

CALL OUT "LORD!"

A new song for the Lord!
Sing it and bless God's name,
everyone, everywhere!
Tell the whole world
God's triumph day to day,
God's glory, God's wonder.

Proclaim the Lord, you nations,
praise the glory of God's power,
praise the glory of God's name!
Bring gifts to the temple,
bow down, all the earth,
tremble in God's holy presence.

Tell the nations, "The Lord rules!"
As the firm earth is not swayed,
nothing can sway God's judgment.

Let heaven and earth be glad,
the sea and sea creatures roar,
the field and its beasts exult.

Then let the trees of the forest sing
before the coming of the Lord,
who comes to judge the nations,
to set the earth aright,
restoring the world to order.

—*from Psalm 96*

Anna Kate was just a baby when her three older siblings began a new school year. Abram was a fourth-grader, Elisabeth a second-grader and Mary Margaret was in kindergarten. I remember that September because I was, for the first time in many years, home alone with an infant. And I was looking forward to long, peaceful times of morning prayer. Anna Kate still took a morning nap and hadn't yet begun to talk. I figured by Christmas I might be levitating

through the kitchen like some medieval mystic, so high were my
hopes for holy peace and quiet.

It's a curious thing: When parents of our acqaintance reach the fourth or fifth child they stop coaxing their tiny babies to sit up or crawl or walk early. They want them to do all those necessary tasks, of course, but the sense of urgency is gone. "Don't bother," I can recall telling Andrew and Anna Kate as they strained to pull up on the edge of a coffee table, "I'll tell you if something worth walking for comes along." I never had much success with this laissez-faire approach to large motor skill development. There were always older children clapping and cheering every attempt at infant independence, always some adored someone modeling the delights of free movement.

So we weren't far into autumn before Anna Kate abandoned her morning nap and learned to pull up on me as I sat cross-legged on the floor in prayer. She would grab whatever skin or bit of clothing was handiest and use me as a brace to move from a sitting to a standing position. Her tiny fingers holding tight, she would sway in a ferocious contest between precarious balance and determined gravity, laughing at the sensation of height and power that was suddenly and wondrously hers. She never stood upright long, and she never stopped trying to regain the position, scrambling for a fresh fingerhold even as she plopped onto the floor. I learned to pray positioned like a top in its last drowsy rotations: slowly dipping now left, now right, coming upright and dipping again — ruled not by the earth's movements but by Anna Kate's.

My mother once described our family as "the mouthiest bunch I ever saw; every lasting one of you has an opinion." Which is why I grew even warier of early verbal facility than of physical precocity. Here again I was subverted in my quest for quiet by older children who delighted in teaching the babies in their care to talk. Abram devoted months of precious after-school time to coaching little Anna Kate in the art of pointing at her head while saying sweetly, "No brains." It always made him laugh, which always made her say it again. The children were aided in this by their father, whose day job is talking to grown-ups. He longed for some baby-babble at the end of the day. It was Martin who taught Andrew to say "two," just that, "two." Then he devised lengthy, complicated math problems for the older children to pose to their baby brother.

The answer, of course, to every problem was "two." This parlor trick occupied Papa and his band for months; the attention convinced Andrew to learn to say more and more words.

No sooner had Anna Kate learned her unsteady stance than she began to talk. "Mama," she said, over and over, all day long, "Mama." She said "Mama" laughing and "Mama" sobbing and "Mama" softly as she went to sleep. She screamed "Mama" when she couldn't see me and posed "Mama?" as a question when she encountered the unfamiliar and wanted a name to attach to the wonder. Anna Kate sang "Mama," a tuneless accompaniment for car rides and stroller outings. She shouted "Mama" for the sheer pleasure and power of volume, letting the syllables "Ma-Ma-Ma-Ma" fill the air with the sound of speech, her speech, speech people understood and to which they, or at least I (and who else mattered then?), responded. She squealed "Mama" when I tickled her and kissed the curve of her neck and blew on her tummy. She called "Mama" again and again as I opened my lips and tried to proclaim God's praise.

I am not a person to whom God speaks often. Either that or I am not a person who listens very well. Still, I remember that year, for God spoke to me one morning as I attempted to peel Anna Kate off my body and shush her just long enough to make it through the opening hymn and a psalm or two. If the psalm that morning was not number 96, it was one very much like it, a psalm that keeps repeating itself: "Proclaim the Lord, you nations/ praise the glory of God's power/ praise the glory of God's name!" "Lord, Lord, Lord" the psalm sings, "glorious God, holy God, majestic God" the psalm sings. And it is then that I recall hearing, not in words like those I "hear" over the telephone but in my heart, these words:

> *Look at your child. Listen to her. She calls for you*
> *day and night, in joy and in sorrow. Your name*
> *is ever on her lips. She calls for you first, last and*
> *always. Do not be impatient with her, but learn*
> *from the child what I desire from you.*

Scholars write of Hebrew prosody, a parallel form of poetry in which a statement is made and then restated in the next line. "A new song for the Lord!" is the command; "Sing it and bless God's name, everyone, everywhere," the restatement. C. S. Lewis calls it "a very pure example of what all pattern, and therefore all art, involves. The principle of art has been defined by someone as 'the same in the other.' Thus in a country dance you take three steps and then three steps again. That is the same. But the first three steps are to the right and the second three to the left. That is the other."

Parents of small children know about statement and restatement, though it often seems more like a slam dance than a country dance. We hear our words come back to us and we are surprised by the sound of them on another's lips. When our first three children were babies together they passed ear infections and tonsillitis back and forth. We were sick-bound for weeks one winter, and my tolerance for flowing noses was wearing thin. So when the children began quarrelling at lunch, I, the resident peacemaker, broke down and started yelling, "Stop it! Stop it! Stop it!" I seem to recall jumping up and down to punctuate. When I calmed down, I apologized and thought no more of it until I heard them later, at play. Elisabeth proposed a round of "house," with herself as the mother, Abram as the father and Mary Margaret alternating the roles of child and dog. That settled, Elisabeth began leaping about the room, waving her hands wildly and shouting, "Stop it! Stop it! Stop it!"

But when the looking glass is tilted slightly, the results can be wondrous. Anna Kate's cries, her "Mama, Mama, Mama," showed me "the same in the other," a kind of mirror for the devotion to which the psalms call us. Is there good news and rejoicing? Call out "Lord!" Is there trouble and confusion? Call out "Lord!" There is no sacred world standing over and against a profane one. There is not one world in which the appropriate cry for help is to the loan officer or psychiatrist and another in which the appropriate cry for help is to God. All creation — all thought and action, all desire and dread — everything belongs to God, rests under the mercy of God. Babies call to us for the septic business of dirty diapers and the sublime work of blowing soap bubbles on the back porch. In all of it they call our names.

Elsewhere in the scriptures Jesus asks the disciples to look at a little child and learn the way in which they — and we — are called to walk. We are not told exactly what the child in the story is doing. Perhaps she was calling the name of her comforter, the source of her nourishment and safety, her teacher and protector, her companion and guide. Perhaps she was calling the name of the one who taught her to name all things, the world and herself in it. Perhaps she was calling the name of her mother, just as we, morning by morning, as the psalmist bids us, call upon the name of the Beloved:

The Three who are over me,
The Three who are below me,
The Three who are above me here,
The Three who are above me yonder,
The Three who are in the earth,
The Three who are in the air,
The Three who are in the heaven,
The Three who are in the great pouring sea.

—*from the* Carmina Gadelica

CHAPTER 5

LET THEM ALL PRAISE

Let there be praise:
from depths of the earth,
from creatures of the deep.

Fire and hail, snow and mist,
storms, winds,
mountains, hills,
fruit trees and cedars,
wild beasts and tame,
snakes and birds,

princes, judges,
rulers, subjects,
men, women,
old and young,
praise, praise the holy name,
this name beyond all names.

God's splendor above the earth,
above the heavens,
gives strength to the nation,
glory to the faithful,
a people close to the Lord.
Israel, let there be praise!

—from Psalm 148

I'm sitting at a reading table in the resource center of my son Andrew's elementary school. It is my day to be "mother helper," and the children are spending their first few "settling in" moments telling me about last night's Halloween adventures. They are eager to talk to me because we share a predilection for what Katie, sitting next to me, calls "getting out of your own boring self" and dressing up as someone — or something — else. I had shown up at the class party the day before dressed as I dress every Halloween — as a witch in green makeup, sporting blacked-out teeth and curved plastic talons and wearing a pointed black hat atop a stringy, synthetic black wig. I came screeching and cackling; "doing all the voices," Andrew says approvingly. I came with refreshments: "eyeballs" in Tupperware. The eyeballs are actually made of lemon gelatin molded in rounded ice cube trays and adorned with blueberry pupils; but we don't discuss that. It is much more satisfying in the second grade to live with the imagined revulsion of chewing and swallowing gelatinous human tissue.

Their stories are familiar ones of canvassing our lighted and decorated neighborhood with parents and friends in search of the generous householders who are handing out "whole Baby Ruths" and not the miserly miniature snack bars — or worse, small boxes of raisins — that most mothers buy. But soon the talk turns to breathless "did you hears?" and we are deep in tales of roving gangs beating up trick-or-treaters and stealing their candy, of depraved adults coating gummy worms with insecticide and burying razor blades in taffy apples. The children have heard of them: that old woman somebody knows in Denver who has a pantry full of arsenic-filled baby food jars, a "weird guy" somewhere, the children forget where, who gives out stickers laced with LSD. None of them encountered the real ghouls; none of them knows anyone who has, but they have heard, they have been warned.

So I am not surprised, later in the day when the children are writing their journal entries on "What I Did on Halloween," to be asked by one little girl, "How do you spell 'Penrose Community

Hospital'?" That autumnal rite, the X-raying of the Halloween candy, had found its way into her recounting of the festivities and will be a part of the memories this generation hands on to the next: the annual high-tech search for rat poisons and rusty nails in the Milky Way bars.

I ask the children if they saw any of this Halloween cruelty. Turns out all they saw were the acts of kindness, large and small, which typically mark the day around here. Andrew, who has been carrying on an over-the-fence love affair with the German grandmother next door since he was born ("Hello, shveetheart," Dorothea sings out whenever she sees him), can always count on a special treat put aside just for him when he crosses to her house in the gathering dusk of All Hallow's Eve. Other children have similar stories: of the retired music professor from the local college who sits in his darkened foyer and plays "Funeral March of a Marionette" on his clarinet while his wife dons a gorilla mask and hands out candy to the delighted children and their nostalgic parents, the parents old enough to remember the theme song from "The Alfred Hitchcock Show."

The need for an Alien, a Stranger, an Other is strong and early born; the need for a gulf between Us and Them is intense and easily learned. Somewhere, people — not people we know, but lots of them, somewhere — routinely spike the popcorn balls with toxins and casually strip small Simbas of their lion masks. Somewhere there is a world — we think it looks like the pictures of East St. Louis, South Central Los Angeles or the South Bronx that we see on the nightly news — where grace has vanished and no trace of the holy is to be found. We hear of children disappearing there, of babies shot in their cribs as they sleep, and it does not trouble us overmuch. That's how it is where the Others live and rule, and we must guard against them. We must be able to identify them as aliens and strangers. We must avoid them. We suspect our town is next, and a child disappearing from our town would raise an outcry, would stir outrage in our hearts. We must protect our own. "Lots of people," one grave-faced little girl told me, "put mean things in their candy."

The psalms are not given over to gauzy glimpses of the happy human family. Somewhere there *are,* the psalmist acknowledges, sea monsters and wild animals — creatures who kill for food. Dinner could be us. There are rulers of the earth and princes who govern, names on a list soaked with the blood of their victims. But just as

the psalmist does not distinguish between the animate — "Praise
God, men, women, old, young" — and the inanimate — "Praise
God, sun and moon" — neither does the psalmist acknowledge a
godless creation, anyone or anything outside the realm of God's
worship and God's grace. "They" are commanded, alongside "Us,"
to declare the glory of God and all of God's works. "You creatures
that crawl and fly" (as one translation has Psalm 148:10) includes
both the bat and the cockroach, the snow goose and the ladybug.
People gather gratefully to watch Canadian geese soar south for the
winter but cringe at flocks of bats flying out into the night. We
delight in a ladybug making its way along our fingers but shudder at
the sight of a cockroach skittering out from under the kitchen sink.
In an animated Disney movie, as the smallest child can tell you, bats

or cockroaches might be villains or comic relief, but neither will ever be the love interest; they are Other.

And it is not just the creepy-crawly things that make us squirm but the monsters that fill us with loathing and revulsion that are somehow not only under the reign of God (subjection we can understand) but part of the endless chorus of creation singing God's praise. Not only do I fail to understand this order of things, I do not accept it. I picture offering the kiss of peace to a cockroach or sitting and sharing a pew and a songbook with a confessed rapist. Worse — that is, more embarrassing because it is no act of imagination but a weekly truth — I think of some of the people in my downtown parish community — unwashed, their teeth unbrushed, the sores on their skin open and untended — who take the cup from

their lips before I take it to my own. I take and drink because I must.
Drinking after another is an intimate act. No one of us, no matter
how thirsty, drains the water from a stranger's half-empty glass. We
don't go about a restaurant sampling coffee from strangers' cups.
Drinking after another is an act kept in the family: husbands drink
after wives, mothers after children, brothers after sisters.

So I take and drink, or give the lie to every assenting "Amen"
spoken and sung around the table to which we are invited precisely
as family—brothers and sisters, bound for all time by blood, the blood
of Christ. I take and drink, but not without a guilty glance at the
Other a few pews over, not without hoping he doesn't slip into "my"
line. I take and drink, but not without reflecting gratefully on the
disinfectant qualities of alcohol.

These are disgusting images, humiliating revelations; it is a troubling psalm. There are Others! They are Other to me and to everyone everywhere — except in this psalm which the church sings in morning praise, this psalm with which the church greets the day. There all the created, those we recognize and those we do not, those we accept and those we do not, tell of the wonders of God. In the movie "Places in the Heart," the final scene shows all the characters in church: the living and the dead, the murdered and his murderer, and those who mourn them. Seated together in the pews, together they sing, together they receive communion, passing the trays of bread and wine from one hand to another, all hands open and all hands filled. And we, like they, are not given the option of singing apart from the rest. All are to "praise, praise the holy name."

I remember nights in bed with my sister, Marilyn, when she would draw an invisible line down the center of the mattress and forbid me to cross it. In the freedom of sleep we rolled back and forth across our unguarded borders and usually awoke a tangle of entwined arms and legs. Morning prayer beckons us to a different kind of freedom where, in full consciousness, we storm our well-guarded borders. In cleansing, stripping praise, we sing down the boundaries until they are no more. Martin Buber tells this story of a holy man:

> *After the maggid's death, his disciples came*
> *together and talked about the things he had done.*
> *When it was Rabbi Schneur Zalman's turn,*
> *he asked them: "Do you know why our master*

*went to the pond every day at dawn and stayed
there for awhile before coming home again?" They
did not know why. Rabbi Zalman continued:
"He was learning the song with which the frogs
praise God. It takes a very long time to learn
that song."*

It takes a very long time to learn that song, the song with which we sing down the boundaries. Morning by morning, with the three young men of Daniel, we cast off the distinctions of us and them, ours and theirs, clean and unclean, and join in the song with which the frogs and all the created praise God:

Bless God beyond the stars.
Give praise and glory.
Bless God, heaven and earth.
Give praise and glory for ever.

Bless God, angels of God.
Give praise and glory.
Bless God, highest heavens.
Give praise and glory.

Bless God, waters above.
Give praise and glory.
Bless God, spirits of God.
Give praise and glory.

Bless God, sun and moon.
Give praise and glory.
Bless God, stars of heaven.
Give praise and glory for ever.

Bless God, rainstorm and dew.
Give praise and glory.
Bless God, gales and winds.
Give praise and glory.

Bless God, fire and heat.
Give praise and glory.
Bless God, frost and cold.
Give praise and glory.

Bless God, dew and snow.
Give praise and glory.
Bless God, ice and cold.
Give praise and glory.

Bless God, frost and sleet.
Give praise and glory.
Bless God, night and day.
Give praise and glory.

Bless God, light and darkness.
Give praise and glory.
Bless God, lightning and clouds.
Give praise and glory.

Bless God, earth and sea.
Give praise and glory.
Bless God, mountains and hills.
Give praise and glory.

Bless God, trees and plants.
Give praise and glory.
Bless God, fountains and springs.
Give praise and glory.

Bless God, rivers and seas.
Give praise and glory.
Bless God, fishes and whales.
Give praise and glory.

Bless God, birds of the air.
Give praise and glory.
Bless God, beasts of the earth.
Give praise and glory for ever.

Bless God, children of earth.
Give praise and glory.
Bless God, Israel.
Give praise and glory.

Daniel 3:56 – 83

CHAPTER 6

THE THING WITH FEATHERS

Blest be the God of Israel, who comes to set us free;
Who visits and redeems us, who grants us liberty.
The prophets spoke of mercy, of freedom and release;
God shall fulfill that promise and bring the people peace.

God, from the house of David, a child of grace has given;
A savior comes among us to raise us up to heaven.
Before him goes the herald, forerunner in the way,
The prophet of salvation, the harbinger of Day.

On prisoners of darkness the sun begins to rise,
The dawning of forgiveness upon the sinner's eyes.
God guides the feet of pilgrims along the paths of peace.
O bless our God and savior with songs that never cease.

— metrical setting of Luke 1:68 – 79 by James Quinn, SJ

My husband's aunt and uncle married with the expectation of a large family. They came from abundant families and from a time when the phrase "Catholic family" conjured images of institutional-sized gatherings. Yet 15 years passed before they conceived. Fifteen years of expectant longing dissolved into disappointment and, finally, resignation. News of the pregnancy surprised us all and filled every-one but the parents with excitement. They, who had prayed and waited with such hope, were now afraid to hope. For a long time, almost to the safe and happy birth itself, they did not want a baby shower, did not want to set up a nursery, did not want to erect any monuments to glad expectation, the shards of which they, weeping, would have to clear away if the child died — as feared — in the womb or at birth. They were in good company.

Remember Zechariah. When he received the joyous news that after so many years of childlessness he and Elizabeth would bear a son, the scriptures recall not his elation but his skepticism, a skepticism true to a waiting many of us have witnessed and some have borne — a waiting that has outlasted hope. But this angel doesn't bring news of restored fertility alone; there is news of the baby's future as well, and the news is wondrous. After all, many couples are fertile, and the fertility bears fruit to set the parents' teeth on edge.

But the angel tells Zechariah of a child who will be noble and good. The child of Elizabeth and Zechariah is to be called "God is gracious." He is to be the joy and delight of his parents, the angel declares, and great in the sight of the Lord. "Many," the angel tells Zechariah, "will rejoice at his birth."

Zechariah responds to the forecast of every parent's dream (notice the angel neglects to mention that the young John will dress in animal skins, become a noticeably picky eater and end his days in prison) with a reluctant "How can I be sure of this?" Commentators take this to mean that Zechariah wanted a sign, something to grasp, some assurance that he could rejoice in confidence. Zechariah is doubtful: It is late in the day ("I am an old man and my wife is getting on in years") and miracles have not been a regular feature of his life thus far. So Zechariah doubts and is struck mute by the angel.

This movement into silence is as good a description of the closing rhythm of our days and the descent into sleep as we are likely to find. Christians end their days with the extravagant claims of yet another canticle, the Canticle of Simeon. With old Simeon we declare that we can depart in peace because God keeps all promises and has prepared the salvation of all peoples. Now this promise is at odds with the promise of the ten o'clock news that rapes and beatings and fatal car crashes will, like some lunatic convenience store of horrors, be open for business 24 hours a day, seven days a week. "Tune in tomorrow morning," the eager-faced announcer chirps at the terrified cowering in their beds and recliners, "for late-breaking news," that is, the news of the carnage that occurred while we slept.

Whom are we to believe? The angel of the Lord is not on the scene with a videocam and a microphone, standing against the ruins of someone's life. And even those who eschew television news, who have no video boost into suspicion and fear, often — perhaps daily — find themselves at the close of a day that has proved longer than hope. So we sing, or mutter, half-asleep, the ancient words of Simeon. And asking with Zechariah, for whom bad news seemed the safer bet, "How can I be sure of this?" we fall into mute sleep.

What no one knows, and scripture isn't telling, is what happened to Zechariah in the silence. But it is clear that something happens to him. He is changed in the silence and perhaps by the silence. We know he is mute from the announcement of the conception through the pregnancy and delivery, right up to the child's circumcision on the eighth day after birth. Zechariah is silent until he names the child John, "God is gracious." "At that instant," Luke writes, "his power of speech returned and he spoke and praised God." Zechariah breaks the long silence with this exclamation: "Blest be the God of Israel, who comes to set us free."

Mark Searle once wrote about issues surrounding the word of God proclaimed in the Sunday assembly. He said that people need to be prepared to hear.

> *Of course God still acts, and of course he still*
> *speaks, but how would we recognize him? If we*

are waiting for the thunder and lightning of theophany, we will probably be disappointed. God speaks in ways which can be easily overlooked. After all, the Egyptians overlooked the presence of God in the Exodus, and many contemporaries of Jesus thought he was a good man, but they were not expecting to experience him as God incarnate. So why should we expect that God will trumpet his presence for us? May it not be that he speaks in the events and circumstances of our own lives and times and we fail to recognize him? The problem may not be that God is absent or silent, but that we do not know God's language.

Or the problem may be that we are never silent. Until recently, the life of the womb was hidden from us; it was a secret place where the child could grow sheltered from sight. Even in the age of sonograms and amniocentesis, parents have months of quiet company with a child who can be neither seen face to face nor touched. That would seem to be an isolating experience, placing parents and child on opposite shores of knowing, for we relate to one another through speech and hearing, through touch and sight. But instead the hidden months are an intimate time, the mother learning, through the baby's internal thumps and swimmer's kick turns, her unborn child. She guides the father's hands over her swelling belly, teaching him. "There, feel that? She's kicking. Here's her foot, I think." The child grows in silence, and the parents grow, too. They grow in hope.

Even sick at her stomach and throwing up, the mother sometimes finds it hard to believe in the first weeks that a child is truly growing within her. How much harder must it be for the father, who can neither see nor feel what is happening in the hidden womb? As the days pass, hope grows: There is someone there. Somewhere in the silent months of gestation my husband's aunt and uncle grew in hope, daring to believe a child would be born to them, that a child of grace is indeed given. Somewhere in the silent months, Zechariah came to believe that the word of God, in all its extravagance, would be revealed and fulfilled, that God is gracious and may be known.

The long work of growing in hope is not an experience peculiar to biological parents. We have friends who have been waiting for eight years to adopt a child. They are in a support group of prospective adoptive parents and they are the only couple not to have received a child. During Advent the husband told me, "We are learning what it means to wait in silence, to wait for that which is hidden to be revealed." They are gestating, too, though the nature of what is being born in them, around them, for them, to them has not yet turned and disclosed a discernible face.

Emily Dickinson wrote:

> *Hope is the thing with feathers*
> *That perches in the soul*
> *And sings the tunes without the words . . .*

It may be that the language of God is the tune "without the words," silence. Dickinson doesn't speak of hope as having no sound, just as we cannot speak of silence as the absence of sound. There is a tune, but it is unexpected; it grows, not out of words or out of any known melody, but out of silence. Those of us who live in Colorado go to the mountains in part to seek the tune without the words, to seek silence.

When our family goes to the mountains, there is always a moment when one of us turns to the others and says, "Listen." What we are listening to, listening for, is the silence. And the longer we listen, the more is revealed: the rubber-toy squeak of a marmot; the wind through the aspens, the leaves making a sound like rice paper wind chimes; the sound of our breaths, lost and caught again at 9,000 feet above the distant seas. Those sounds are everywhere in the

mountains, but we have to be still; we have to stop moving and talking, stop clicking shutters and clucking tongues in order to hear what
the silence reveals. And sometimes the silence is so profound that
what we hear, all we hear, is the rush of blood through arteries and
the air drawn in and released, faster as we pause to listen and then
slower as we sit in stillness. We hear things there in the mountains
that we hear nowhere else. And so we return, summer after summer.

Wise men and women counsel us daily to seek silence; we
seldom do. So God, the good and gracious one, seeks it for us. Sleep
seems such an inconvenience to the young and the strong and to the
busy. It strikes us as some ancient adaptive debris, like the appendix,
which is no longer useful. Biographies of the powerful often mention the disciplined way in which these leaders shun sleep, not for

meditation and prayer like the mystics and holy ones but in order to cram more work and work product into each 24-hour period. With a fax machine, 2:00 AM loses its closed quality: For somebody, somewhere, it's business hours.

It may be that the silence of night, coming to us in the physical necessity of sleep, is given, even imposed upon those of us who would not choose it otherwise. Like all mothers I am well acquainted with the whine "But I'm not sleepy!" which signals the descent into fatigue-induced hysteria. And like all mothers, I have promised children, whose dearest desire is to "be big," that it is only during sleep that children grow taller. I have no idea whether this is true. I suspect it is a piece of mother-lore I gleaned from my own mother, who knew she wouldn't be getting any rest until I was tucked in for the night. But it makes sense to me that growth requires attention on that process alone, its energies untapped by the work of play and exploration. The experience of carrying my unborn children in the womb has taught me that some growth can occur only in silence.

Perhaps it is in silence, when our minds are freed from distraction to focus on all that the silence reveals in dreams and other unconscious ramblings, that we begin to hear "the thing with feathers" singing in our souls and so learn again the language of God, the language of hope, the language of silence. It is out of the silence that Zechariah sings. It is out of the silence of the night that the fast from words is broken with the glad cry to the God of Israel, "who visits and redeems us, who grants us liberty."

O sweet and loving God,
When I stay asleep too long,
Oblivious to your many blessings,
Then, please, wake me up,
And sing to me your joyful song.
It is a song without noise or notes.
It is a song of love beyond words,
Of faith beyond the power of human telling,
I can hear it in my soul,
When you awaken me to your presence.

—Mechtild of Magdeburg

CHAPTER 7

HOW CAN I KEEP FROM SINGING?

My life flows on in endless song
    above earth's lamentations.
I hear the real though far-off hymn
    that hails a new creation.

Through all the tumult and the strife,
    I hear that music ringing;
It sounds and echoes in my soul;
    How can I keep from singing?

No storm can shake my inmost calm,
While to that Rock I'm clinging,
Since Love is Lord of heaven and earth,
How can I keep from singing?

— Quaker hymn

Small children sing. They sing their days. They sing the blues about taking a bath:

> Mama made me take a bath.
> I had to wash my hair and I don't like it.
> Soap gets in my nose and makes me sneeze
> and soap gets in my eyes and makes me cry

and soap gets in my mouth and makes me throw up
and Mama says stop it.

They sing of new babies, as I once heard our Anna Kate sing softly to the tiny brother who lay, blissfully uncomprehending the lyrics, before her in his bassinet:

Go home. Go home.
Go home, little baby, go home.
It's time for you to go home.
Go home, little baby, go home.

They sing of their triumphs:

> I use the potty all the time.
> I used to wear diapers but now I don't because I'm big.
> I use the potty all the time like the big kids.

And of their delights:

> We're having chocolate pudding for supper;
>> it's my favorite.
> Chocolate pudding is my favorite thing in the
>> whole world.
> I could eat a bazillion, quatrillion, hundred
>> chocolate puddings.
> I'm gonna ask for seconds and thirds and thousands!

Small children sing songs they learn at preschool and at church and from their parents, too, but they would never confine their repertoire to a group of already composed songs. And they would never confine their singing to designated singing places and times, as do adults. We know to haul ourselves to our feet and strain through the "Star-Spangled Banner" before a football game. We know to stand and sing the entrance hymn at church, though we're miffed if the organist drags us through all the verses. But for the most part, we've learned that singing is best left to professionals; they are to sing and we are to watch and listen.

Not so for children: Whatever exists in the world, either seen or unseen, children will sing about it. Finding oneself alive in the world is reason enough to sing. There are songs for dead pets and songs for spending the night away from home and songs for older brothers and sisters who won't let you touch their things. There are songs for birthdays — "Happy birthday to me!" — and songs for the first solo street crossing and songs for going swimming. Sheer pleasure at being prompts our Andrew to belt out "Chantilly Lace," finishing with an exuberant animal growl, "Oh, baby, you know what I like!" and then telling me with a grin, "Legos!" They cannot keep from singing.

If we think of the hours of the day as corresponding to the seasons of our lives, then morning is clearly newborn — the sun just rising, the work of the day still before us, the hurts and hard words not yet inflicted or received. We open our eyes on possibilities and our hearts to fresh chances. Perhaps this is the day I will start walking a mile or holding my tongue with an elderly parent or a teenage child; perhaps this is the day I will find the courage to leave or to stay, to begin or to end. It may not be — the texts of evening and night prayer suggest we will fail in much the same way day after day, just as Andrew may not become a spelunker or an archeologist (a la Indiana Jones), as he currently vows. Life will help him narrow his choices; the demands of the day will help us reevaluate ours. We will be worn down by the world, by the hours before us; we will come to the end weary and seeking solace and safety. But the morning dawns on three glad realities, the only three we need immediately consider: The world is still turning; we are still alive on it; God is Lord of all. Life — God's gift, given again — that's what we sing and bless

and give thanks for in the morning — that there is still life and that
it is still ours.

In the first Hollywood musicals, there was always a set-up for a song-and-dance number: The kids were putting on a show in the barn or the hoofers were entertaining the troops. There was some plausible reason for people to be singing and jumping about. Then came "Singing in the Rain" and Gene Kelly's famous reply to the cop on the beat who asks him what he's doing, twirling around street-lamps and warbling for all the world like a four-year old in a mud puddle, "Doo-doo-doo-doodoo-doo-doo-doo." "I'm singing," Kelly croons, like a child at play, "just singing and dancing in the rain." When children sing, I think it is, in part, to add the proper gloss of wonder that mere spoken words cannot contain, the gloss of wonder to what adults dismiss as ordinary, everyday — like rain. Kelly's reply spoken to the officer might have sounded smart-alecky — "What's it look like I'm doing?" But sung, the wonder and playfulness and delight is all there, spread out like the magic carpet of fairy tales. We want to step upon the carpet, to sing and dance.

I cannot remember toilet training as a child, but I remember the faces of my own toddlers who stayed dry through a nap and then through a night; it warranted a song. I cannot remember how good chocolate pudding can taste, but I know from the delighted faces of those in my care that its praises must be sung. To awake to life and light merits, demands, a song.

The psalmist, like a child singing her days, takes the obvious and sets it to music:

This is the day the Lord made,
Let us rejoice and be glad.

I will thank you, my God,
I will praise you highly.
Give thanks, the Lord is good,
God's love is forever.

　　— from Psalm 118

　　There is no information as to what this day holds: fair weather or foul, good fortune or ill, sickness or health. We can imagine a song in honor of winning the lottery, but this is praise of what we've come to take for granted: God has said to the sun, "Get up and do it again." That, says the psalmist, is cause for rejoicing.

The psalmist looks out upon the world illuminated by the risen sun and finds reason to sing. Not because humankind and animals are doing something novel or unexpected but because they are doing what they do every morning:

> *Lord our God,*
> *the whole world tells*
> *the greatness of your name.*
> *Even the babble of infants*
> *declares your strength.*
> *I see your handiwork in the heavens.*

Lord our God,
the whole world tells
the greatness of your name.
— from Psalm 8

Not just songs but accompanied songs belong to the praise of the morning. Instruments, played with care and skill, belong to the praise of the morning. The most glorious music we know belongs not to the record companies and Broadway stages alone but to the praise of the One by whose breath the heavens were made:

Praise God on the harp,
with ten-string lyre
sing to the Lord.

Sing God a new song.
Play music to match
your shout of joy.

God speaks: the heavens are made;
God breathes: the stars shine.
God bottles the waters of the sea
and stores them in the deep.

God speaks: the world is;
God commands: all things appear.

— from Psalm 33

Traditional Christian hymnody sounds the same note as the psalms:

From all who dwell below the skies,
Let the Creator's praise arise:
Let the Redeemer's name be sung,
Through every land by every tongue.

Holy, holy, holy, Lord God Almighty;
Early in the morning a song shall rise to thee.

Why? The composers don't say, and, one suspects, might find the question silly. Why praise? Why cry out "Holy, holy, holy"? Because God is the Creator and Redeemer, the Almighty One. Because God is, and, early in the morning — this morning at least — so are we. How can we keep from singing?

Sunrise is an event that calls forth solemn music in the very depth of human nature, as if one's whole being had to attune itself to the cosmos and praise God for the new day, praise God in the name of all creatures that ever were or ever will be. I look at the rising sun and feel that now upon me falls the responsibility of seeing what all my ancestors have seen, in the Stone Age and before it, praising God before me. When the sun rises each one of us is summoned by the living and the dead to praise God.

— Thomas Merton

THAT WE SHALL BE ABLE TO SEE

Bless, O Christ, my face.
Let my face bless everything.
Bless, O Christ, my eyes.
Let my eyes bless all they see.

— morning blessings

Claire was a member of our parish and a faithful participant in an adult education class I teach there on Sunday mornings. She had children the ages of two of my own and was a woman — like me, I would have said — with years before her, years before her hips or heart gave out. Because that's the measure: People my age don't land on the parish list of intentions for the sick and the dying. We take care of the sick and the dying, carrying the meals to the house and laying out the funeral dinners. We shake our heads and make soft clucking sounds over the news that surgeons performed a triple bypass on this or that octogenarian, and declare our firm intention that when we get to that age, "they can just let me go." "That age" being, we think, distant, hard to imagine, let alone see, but an age whose demands we're sure we'll master.

We sound like the teenagers in my care who announce with youthful conviction all the things they will always/never do. In a rush to get out of the house one morning, I found myself sharing the bathroom with Elisabeth, a blooming 18. She looked at me appraisingly, a certain pitying wonderment in her eyes, and said simply, "I will never allow that to happen to me." I wished her well. I still do. And I advised her that, if she ever finds a way to stop "that," she should drop out of college immediately and begin selling the formula, which will bring her riches and renown.

And so, I'm sure it must be with the older women of our parish watching us, those older women who live what we younger ones deny: the winding down of all their days. We will never allow *that* to happen to us. And if, indeed, we die — in some distant future — we will die with a style our elders seem not to have mastered.

When illness and death come to people our age, people with dependent children and unpaid mortgages, people who haven't yet been to France or taken up the piano as they promised to do once the kids were grown, we are angry and aggrieved. "It isn't fair," we say; "she has so much to live for," we cry. And in the cry we hear the slow, or perhaps not so slow, inexorable unwinding of our own life spring. And we are afraid.

It was fear I felt when I heard the diagnosis of Claire's cancer — fear and anger. We both had children entering middle school in the fall, and everyone knows how difficult the middle school years can be for children. Claire — and by extension, me — was needed. This dying, I thought bitterly, it's really not a good time.

Claire struggled to live, prayed to live, and we prayed with her. Radical surgery and chemotherapy and radiation and radiation sickness, and then the news that Claire had gone into the local hospice to die. We heard on Sunday morning; that afternoon I went to see her. I went, ruddy and bursting with health — desperate to confirm my health. I went to pity and to commiserate, and to absorb some of the rage I knew she must feel against God and the failed doctors and her unreliable body. I knew that in her place I would be angry.

When I entered Claire's room she was seated in a velour lounger, a chair with no sharp edges to snag an IV line or bruise the unpadded flesh of her frame. She rose and embraced me. "Melissa," she said, her arms about me tight, "God loves us very much." I had not intended to stay longer than courtesy demanded. But with her unexpected greeting I knew I would remain that day and come again, if Claire permitted it. For I was Claire's teacher, but Claire became my master. She became the comforter and I the comforted. I came to help and stayed to learn, in the presence of this dying woman, how to bless life, how to "let my eyes bless all I see" even when those eyes open onto the landscape of one's deathbed. For if I were to take a word association test and hear the word "blessing," I would not answer "cancer" or "death." When I hear the word "blessing," I think of my husband, our children, my friends, my health, that which I know to be good. I wasn't sure what Claire meant when she spoke from that ravaged body, "God loves us very much," but I wanted to find out.

Father Alexander Schmemann wrote of men and women that we, of all creation, have been given the work of blessing God for the food and the life God gives us. We alone are privileged to respond to God's blessing with our blessing. Schmemann connects the act of blessing with the task given to Adam in the garden, the task of naming all that lives. Schmemann writes:

*To name a thing is to manifest the meaning
and value God gave it, to know it as coming from
God and to know its place and function within
the cosmos created by God. To name a thing . . .
is to bless God for it and in it . . . to bless
God . . . to thank him [is] to see the world as
God sees it.*

To ask Christ to bless our eyes, then, is to ask first for the eyes of Christ. We must see rightly and name truly — no lies allowed, even the kindest and most comfortable — if we are to bless. To bless a child is to know the meaning and value God gave her, as God's gift, not our property. To bless food ("Bless us, O Lord, and these thy gifts which we are about to receive from thy bounty") is to know it as coming from God and not from oneself. To bless life, and death, is to know its place and function within the cosmos created by God. To bless is not necessarily to approve. To bless is to give over approval. To bless is to put down the lenses of our own fashioning and to ask if we might, instead, look through God's eyes to see the startling harmony of all things, those we can accept and those we cannot, related in ways undreamt and unimagined.

When our oldest child, Abram, was a baby, his papa took him outside to gaze at the harvest moon. I can see them still: Abram, hushed and wondering, Martin pointing to the night sky and murmuring, "There's the moon, Abram. Can you see? The moon." It was Abram's first moon, his first time to be awake and aware in the night.

He had no words for the experience, no memories of similar experiences with which to compare this one. We have no way of knowing what he thought or felt. The whole experience must have seemed strange: Where has the light gone? What is this dimmer brightness hanging where the familiar ball usually burns? But however confused or anxious Abram felt, he did not cry or hide himself in Martin's arms. His father was calm and glad and warm and welcoming. His father was near and Abram knew, knows, the safety of those arms. Abram first saw the night sky and the moon suspended in the heavens through his father's eyes, saw it as Papa sees, and he was not afraid.

Claire knew she was dying. She named these days for what they were: her last. She had not wanted to die. She wanted what every mother wants: to raise her children, her Celeste and Maurice, to honorable adulthood. She wanted to grow old with her husband, and with him to welcome grandchildren. She had worked hard to get well, and she wept to leave them behind when it became clear she would never be well again. But no fear, no worry, could destroy what she knew more deeply and truly than her fears: the goodness of God. Somewhere she had learned to see the world as God sees it. She faced death the way a beloved child will follow a parent out of bed and into the darkness of a winter night. The child may be confused, wondering, tearful and afraid. Still, she knows this: Her father loves her, her mother loves her; if they ask her to go, it is safe to follow. So Claire faced death, called it by its true name, and blessed it.

It is the same morning sun to which all our eyes open, but our opened eyes filter the light through the prism of individual

experience and temperament. The prayer of believers in the morning, though, seems to neither acknowledge nor particularly value
the touches we've learned to polish to the sharp-edged sheen we
bring to the marketplace and the workplace. Our eyes are commanded, wherever they open and upon whatever scene, to "bless all
they see." What can this mean? The morning psalm-prayer for the
first week of the cycle of ordinary time reminds us:

> *Lord, all justice and all goodness come from*
> *you; you hate evil and abhor lies. Lead us, your*
> *servants in the path of your justice, so that all*
> *who hope in you may rejoice with the church and*
> *in Christ.*

To bless all we see, to see as the Lord of all justice and goodness sees, is not to blind ourselves to the wounds of the world. We praise the God of the Exodus in morning prayer, the One who sees the affliction of the people of God, the One who hears their cry.

For most of us, the first encounter with the larger world comes through the "news," the recital of affliction and outcry: car wrecks and shootings and little wars in little lands, told morning by morning, with only the dates and names changing from day to day. It would be impossible to hear clearly what we hear, and to read rightly what we read, and not believe that there are wolves along the road. Schmemann writes that seeing and naming and blessing are related. We must first see the world as it is, calling it and all we encounter in it, by true names before we can bless, either blessing God *for* the thing or blessing God *in* the thing.

I don't know if Claire blessed God for death; I know she blessed God in it. She believed that in baptism she had become the temple of God where, in life or in death, God's spirit dwells. Claire believed that in God's mercy the faithful departed find rest. She had no words of her own for this experience, and no memory of a similar experience on which to draw. We die only once; for each of us it is the first time. She had the words of the faithful, the words with which Christians through the ages have ushered their beloved into death. And she clung to God, the safety of whose arms she knew, knows. She saw death through God's eyes, and she was not afraid.

Lord, put your hands on our eyes,
That we shall be able to see not only that which is visible,
But also that which is invisible.
Let our eyes be focused,
Not only on that which is present,
But also on that which is to come.
Unseal the heart's vision,
That we may gaze on God in glory.

— Origen

THE MORNING PRAYER OF THE CHURCH

What follows is a brief order of Morning Prayer. It contains the texts that have been the foundation for the church praying at the beginning of the day. A few of these texts used day by day will soon be known by heart. Or a larger portion of these prayers may be read from the book when praying alone or in a community. Daily prayer includes more than words; silence, posture and gesture, along with chant and song, all enter into the ritual.

Introductory verse

Make the sign of the cross and say:

Lord, open my lips.
And my mouth will proclaim your praise.

Invitatory — Psalm 67

Favor and bless us, Lord.
Let your face shine on us,
revealing your way to all peoples,
salvation the world over.

Let the nations sing your praise,
every nation on earth.

The world will shout for joy,
for you rule the planet with justice.
In fairness you govern the nations
and guide the peoples of earth.

Let the nations sing your praise,
every nation on earth.

The land delivers its harvest,
God, our God, has blessed us.

O God, continue your blessing,
may the whole world worship you.

Hymn

This hymn or another morning hymn is sung.

Now that the daylight fills the sky,
We lift our hearts to God on high,
That God in all we do or say,
Would keep us free from harm today.

O Lord, restrain our tongues from strife,
From wrath and anger shield our life;

And guard with watchful care our eyes
That we will choose from all that's wise.

O may our inmost heart be pure,
From thoughts of folly kept secure,
And all our pow'rs devoted be
To deeds of love that keep us free.

So we, when this day's work is o'er,
And shades of night return once more,
Our path of trial safely trod,
Shall give the glory to our God.

All praise to God the Father be,
And praise the Son eternally,
Whom with the Spirit we adore,
One God alone, for evermore.
—*Jam lucis orto sidere,* eighth century

Psalmody

One or more of these psalms or other psalms assigned to morning prayer may be sung or recited.

Psalm 5

Hear my words, my groans,
my cries for help,
O God my king.
I pray to you, Lord,
my prayer rises with the sun.
At dawn I plead my case and wait.

You never welcome evil, God,
never let it stay.
You hate arrogance
and abhor scoundrels,

you detest violence
and destroy the traitor.

But by your great mercy
I enter your house
and bend low in awe
within your holy temple.

In the face of my enemies
clear the way,
bring me your justice.

Their charges are groundless,
they breathe destruction;

their tongues are smooth,
their throat an open grave.

God, pronounce them guilty,
catch them in their own plots,
expel them for their sins;
they have betrayed you.

But let those who trust you
be glad and celebrate for ever.
Protect those who love your name,
then they will delight in you.

For you bless the just, O God,
your grace surrounds all like a shield.

Psalm 51

Have mercy, tender God,
forget that I defied you.
Wash away my sin,
cleanse me from my guilt.

I know my evil well,
it stares me in the face,
evil done to you alone
before your very eyes.

How right your condemnation!
Your verdict clearly just.
You see me for what I am,
a sinner before my birth.

You love those centered in truth;
teach me your hidden wisdom.
Wash me with fresh water,
wash me bright as snow.

Fill me with happy songs,
let the bones you bruised now dance.
Shut your eyes to my sin,
make my guilt disappear.

154- Creator, reshape my heart,
God, steady my spirit.
Do not cast me aside
stripped of your holy spirit.

Save me, bring back my joy,
support me, strengthen my will.
Then I will teach your way
and sinners will turn to you.

Help me, stop my tears,
and I will sing your goodness.
Lord, give me words
and I will shout your praise.

When I offer a holocaust,
the gift does not please you.
So I offer my shattered spirit;
a changed heart you welcome.

In your love make Zion lovely,
rebuild the walls of Jerusalem.
Then sacrifice will please you,
young bulls upon your altar.

Psalm 85

Lord, you loved your land,
brought Jacob back,

forgot our guilt,
forgave our sins,
swallowed your anger,
your blazing anger.

Bring us back,
saving God.
End your wrath.
Will it stop,
or drag on for ever?

Turn, revive us,
nourish our joy.

Show us mercy,
save us, Lord!

I listen to God speaking:
"I, the Lord, speak peace,
peace to my faithful people
who turn their hearts to me."
Salvation is coming near,
glory is filling our land.

Love and fidelity embrace,
peace and justice kiss.
Fidelity sprouts from the earth,
justice leans down from heaven.

The Lord pours out riches,
our land springs to life.
Justice clears God's path,
justice points the way.

Psalm 146

Hallelujah!

Praise the Lord, my heart!
My whole life, give praise.
Let me sing to God
as long as I live.

Never depend on rulers:
born of earth, they cannot save.
They die, they turn to dust.
That day, their plans crumble.

They are wise who depend on God,
who look to Jacob's Lord,
creator of heaven and earth,
maker of the teeming sea.

The Lord keeps faith for ever,
giving food to the hungry,
justice to the poor,
freedom to captives.

160- The Lord opens blind eyes
and straightens the bent,
comforting widows and orphans,
protecting the stranger.
The Lord loves the just
but blocks the path of the wicked.

Zion, praise the Lord!
Your God reigns for ever,
from generation to generation.
Hallelujah!

Psalm 148

Hallelujah!

Praise the Lord!
Across the heavens,
from the heights,
all you angels, heavenly beings,
sing praise, sing praise!

Sun and moon, glittering stars,
sing praise, sing praise.
Highest heavens, rain clouds,
sing praise, sing praise.

162-   Praise God's name,
        whose word called you forth
        and fixed you in place for ever
        by eternal decree.

        Let there be praise:
        from the depths of the earth,
        from creatures of the deep.

        Fire and hail, snow and mist,
        storms, winds,
        mountains, hills,
        fruit trees and cedars,

wild beasts and tame,

snakes and birds,

princes, judges,
rulers, subjects,
men, women,
old and young,
praise, praise the holy name,
this name beyond all names.

God's splendor above the earth,
above the heavens,
gives strength to the nation,
glory to the faithful,

a people close to the Lord.
Israel, let there be praise!

Canticle of Daniel

See the text on pages 83 – 84.

The Word of God

Here the Bible is read. At the end of the reading, say:

The word of the Lord
Thanks be to God.

Then there is time for silent reflection.

Gospel Canticle

The Canticle of Zechariah (Luke 1:68–79) is sung or recited.

Praise the Lord, the God of Israel,
who shepherds the people and sets them free.

God raises from David's house
a child with power to save.
Through the holy prophets
God promised in ages past
to save us from enemy hands,
from the grip of all who hate us.

The Lord favored our ancestors
recalling the sacred covenant,
the pledge to our ancestor Abraham,
to free us from our enemies,
so we might worship without fear
and be holy and just all our days.

And you, child, will be called
Prophet of the Most High,
for you will come to prepare
a pathway for the Lord
by teaching the people salvation
through forgiveness of their sin.

Out of God's deepest mercy

a dawn will come from on high,

light for those shadowed by death,

a guide for our feet on the way to peace.

Prayers

Prayers of praise and intercession are made, aloud or in silence. At the conclusion, the Our Father is chanted or recited. One of the many prayers that are given in the chapters of this book might also be recited.

Blessing

May the Lord bless us,
protect us from all evil
and bring us to everlasting life.
Amen.

Note: Other resources for Morning Prayer are available from Liturgy Training Publications. These include: Psalms for Morning and Evening Prayer *(the ICEL translation);* Proclaim Praise *(a simple form of Morning and Evening Prayer for each day of the week);* Morning and Evening: A Parish Celebration, *by Joyce Ann Zimmerman.*

.

Verses from "The Whole Earth Shall Cry Glory!" by George Macleod from *HarperCollins Book of Prayers*, compiled by Robert VandeWeyer, © 1993.

Prayer by Saint Catherine of Siena from *The Prayers of Catherine of Siena*, ed. by Suzanne Noffke, copyright © 1983 Paulist Press. Used with permission.

"O God, early in the morning I cry to you" from *Letters and Papers from Prison*, Revised, Enlarged Edition, by Dietrich Bonhoeffer, translated by Reginald Fuller, Frank Clark et al. Copyright © 1953, 1967, 1971 by SCM Press Ltd. Reprinted with permission of Simon & Schuster.

Story of Rabbi Schneur Zalman as told by Martin Buber from *Tales of the Hasidim: The Early Masters*, copyright © 1978 Schocken Books. Used with permission.

Metrical setting of Luke 1:68 – 79 by James Quinn, SJ, copyright © 1969 Selah Publishing Co. Inc., Kingston, New York. Used with permission.

Quote from Thomas Merton from *Conjectures of a Guilty Bystander*, copyright © 1965 Doubleday, Inc. Used with permission.